Learn to Machine Quilt

INTERACTIVE DVD

Wendy Sheppard

Annie's

Machine Quilting Sampler

Skill Level

 BEGINNER

Quilt Size

24" x 24"

Materials

We suggest that you purchase 100 percent cotton fabric in a solid color, batik or muslin to make this sampler. To see your stitches better, choose a dark fabric and light-color thread. Consult the video for more fabric, thread and batting suggestions.

- 2 yards cotton solid*
- 1 yard batting*
- 50–60-wt. quilting thread*
- Basic sewing tools and supplies

*Kona Cotton Solids by Robert Kaufman; Hobbs Tuscany Silk batting; Aurifil Mako 50-wt. 2-ply Egyptian cotton thread were used to make the video sampler quilt.

Essential Machine-Quilting Tools

Below is a list of essential machine-quilting tools that you will need, besides your sewing machine, to machine quilt with success.

- Walking or even-feed sewing machine foot*
- Open-toe embroidery or free-motion quilting foot*
- 80/12 sewing machine needles*
- Water-soluble or heat-erasable fabric markers**
- Quilter's grip gloves
- Teflon mat**
- Spray starch
- Blue painter's masking tape
- Pencil and paper
- Nickel-plated quilting basting pins

*Consult your sewing machine manual for information on the correct type of sewing machine feet and needles for your machine.
** Dritz, Clover and FriXion by Pilot marking tools; Supreme Free-Motion Slider.™

Cutting

1. Cut three 2¼" by fabric width strips from solid for binding.

2. Cut one 24½" square from solid for quilt top.

3. Cut one 28" square from solid for quilt backing.

4. Cut one 28" square from batting.

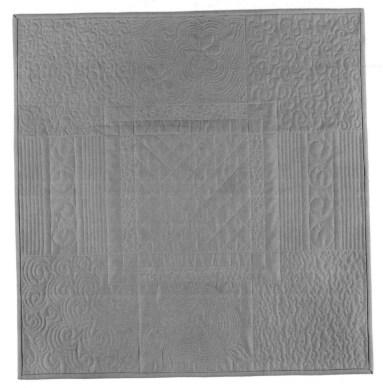

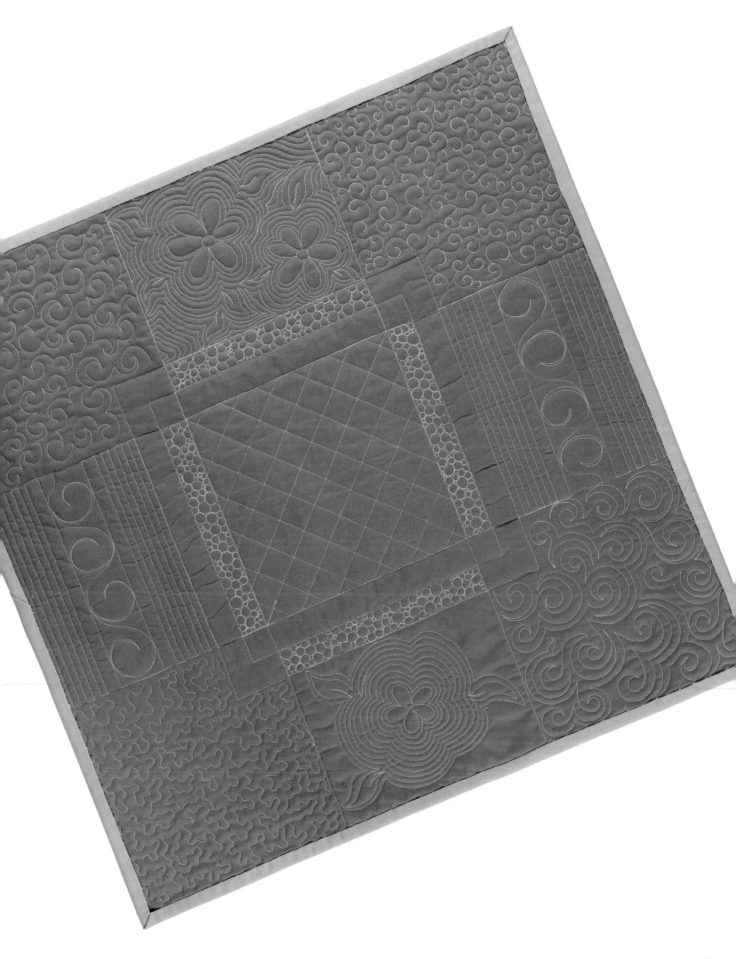

Marking Quilt Top

1. Treat quilt top and backing squares with spray starch following manufacturer's instructions and press. Set aside backing square.

2. Find and mark the center of the quilt top. From this center point, measure 12" out to the outside edges and draw a 24" square using a water-soluble or heat-erasable fabric marker.

3. Measure and mark nine 8" squares within the 24" square referring to Figure 1. *Note: To make it easier to refer to a particular square, the drawing squares have been labeled 1–9.*

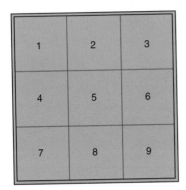

Figure 1

4. Mark a 1"- and 2"-larger square around center square (square 5) as shown in Figure 2.

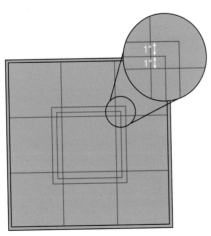

Figure 2

5. Mark square 5 with evenly spaced lines on both diagonals, referring to Figure 3 and the video, to create a diamond crosshatch pattern.

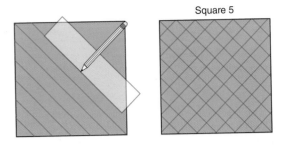

Square 5

Figure 3

6. Mark squares 2 and 8 with lines spaced 2", ½" and ¼" apart referring to Figure 4.

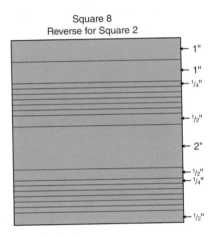

Square 8
Reverse for Square 2

1"
1"
¼"
½"
2"
½"
¼"
½"

Figure 4

Note: Square 8 will look like Figure 4 with 1" sections at top (already marked in step 4); reverse for square 2 with 1" marks at bottom of square.

Making a Quilt Sandwich

1. Tape the backing, wrong side up, to a flat surface with blue painter's masking tape smoothing out all wrinkles.

2. Layer batting and the quilt top, right side up, centered on the backing, again smoothing out all wrinkles in each layer (Figure 5).

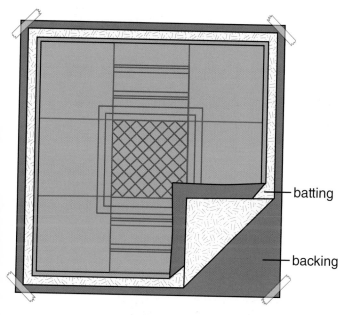

Figure 5

3. Baste the layers together referring to the video for specific basting techniques. Remove masking tape after basting.

Quilting the Sampler Quilt

1. Quilt all straight lines marked on the quilt referring to the video for specifics.

2. Each of the nine squares in the sampler quilt shows a different quilting design that is introduced in the Machine Quilting video. We have included enlarged stitch-path drawings that will help you see how to stitch in the correct directions as shown in the video. Refer to the video for specifics on stitching these quilting designs.

Finishing the Sampler Quilt

1. When quilting is complete, remove any remaining pin or thread basting. Trim batting and backing edges even with raw edges of quilt top.

2. Join binding strips on short ends with diagonal seams to make one long strip; trim seams to ¼" and press seams open.

3. Fold the binding strip in half with wrong sides together along length; press.

4. Sew binding to quilt edges, matching raw edges, mitering corners and overlapping ends. Refer to your favorite quilting manual for specific instructions.

5. Fold binding to the back side and stitch in place to finish. ●

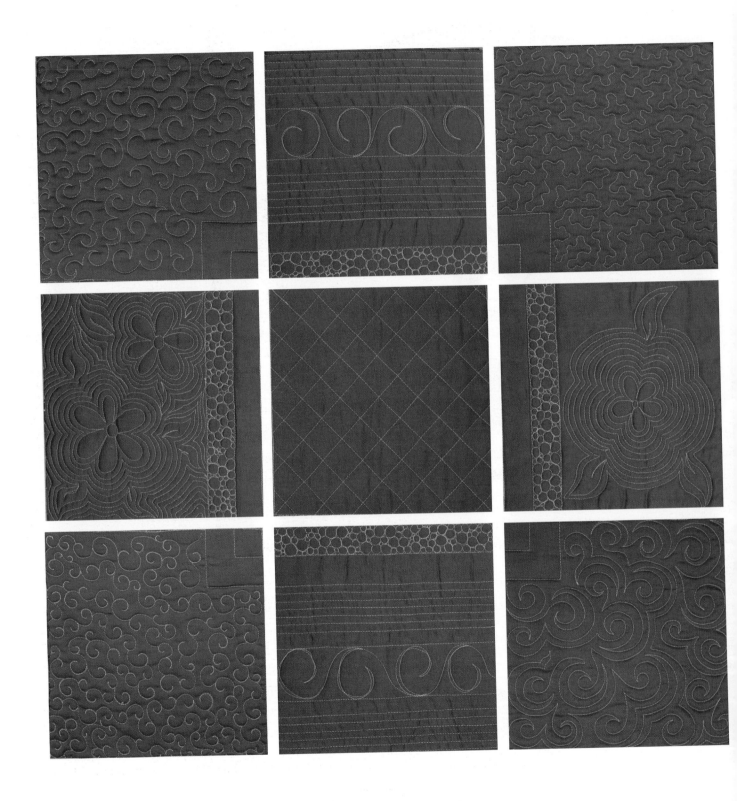

Sampler Quilt
Placement Diagram 24" x 24"

● Start

Jester's Hat Stitch Path
Square 1
This is a swirl technique that stitches a swirl and
proceeds to another swirl without the echoes of the
Allover Swirls pattern.

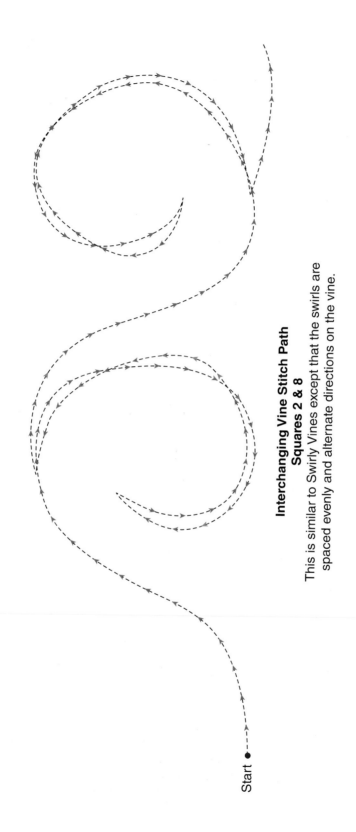

**Interchanging Vine Stitch Path
Squares 2 & 8**
This is similar to Swirly Vines except that the swirls are spaced evenly and alternate directions on the vine.

Start ●

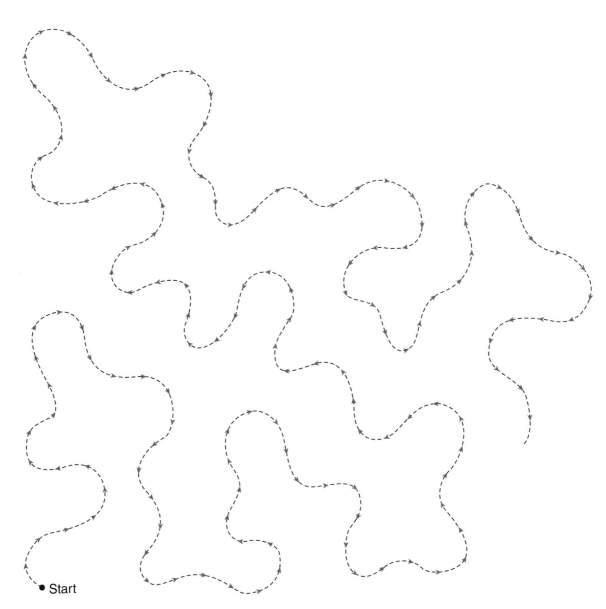

• Start

Stippling Stitch Path
Square 3
Stippling is an allover quilting design, also commonly called meandering, that is a series of randomly stitched curves that typically do not cross. Refer to Stippling in the video.

Double Echo Stitch Path
Square 4
Echo quilting is stitching around a shape—either an appliqué,
a design on the fabric or a stitched design—multiple times, usually an equal
distance apart. This can be done around a single shape or multiple shapes,
creating a ripple effect. Refer to the Echoing section of the video.

● Start

Pebbles Stitch Path
Squares 2, 4, 6 & 8
This design is made up of different-size small circles stitched
closely together. It makes a beautiful background quilting motif.

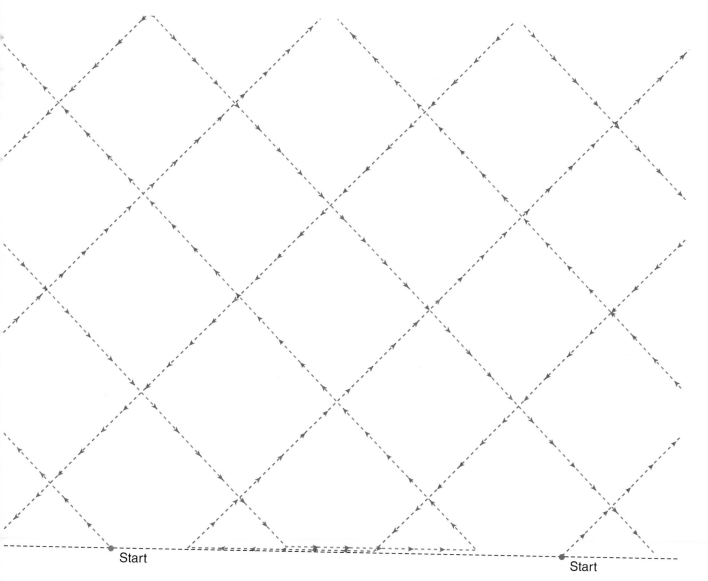

Start

Start

Crosshatch Stitch Path
Square 5
Crosshatch is a straight-line design made from lines stitched an
equal distance apart, in two directions, to create squares or
diamonds. Refer to the Quilting Straight Lines section of the video.

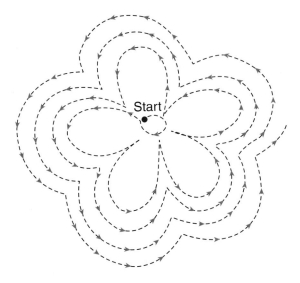

Start

Echo Stitch Path
Square 6
Echo quilting is stitching around a shape—either an appliqué,
a design on the fabric or a stitched design—multiple times usually an equal
distance apart. This can be done around a single shape or multiple shapes
creating a ripple effect. Refer to the Echoing section of the video.

Start ●- - -

Swirly Vines Stitch Path
Square 7
These swirls resemble the tendrils on a vine and can be
close or far apart on the vine and look equally good.

● Start

Allover Swirls Stitch Path
Square 9
An extension of the Echo quilting technique, swirls are stitched,
then echoed before beginning another swirl.
Refer to Allover Swirls in the video.

Annie's® *Learn to Machine Quilt* is published by Annie's, 306 East Parr Road, Berne, IN 46711. Printed in USA. Copyright © 2014 Annie's.
All rights reserved. This publication may not be reproduced in part or in whole without written permission from the publisher.

RETAIL STORES: If you would like to carry this pattern book or any other Annie's publication, visit AnniesWSL.com.

Every effort has been made to ensure that the instructions in this pattern book are complete and accurate. We cannot, however, take responsibility for human error, typographical mistakes or variations in individual work. Please visit AnniesCustomerCare.com to check for pattern updates.

ISBN: 978-1-57367-495-9

1 2 3 4 5 6 7 8 9